Holiday Magic Books

St. Patrick's Day

MAGIC

by James W. Baker
pictures by George Overlie

Lerner Publications Company Minneapolis

To the Irish...and to the English, the French, the Dutch, the Germans, the Turks, the Indians, the Pakistanis, the Tunisians, the Chinese, and all the nationalities for whom it was my pleasure to entertain with magic...for convincing me that magic is truly a universal language that helps promote understanding among the peoples of the world.

Library of Congress Cataloging-in-Publication Data

Baker, James W., 1926-
  St. Patrick's Day magic/by James W. Baker; pictures by George Overlie.
      p.   cm. —(Holiday magic books)
  Summary: Directions for ten magic tricks with a St. Patrick's Day theme.
  ISBN 0-8225-2234-9
  1. Tricks—Juvenile literature. 2. Saint Patrick's Day—Juvenile literature.   [1. Magic tricks. 2. Saint Patrick's Day.] I. Overlie, George, ill. II. Title. III. Title: Saint Patrick's Day magic. IV. Series: Baker, James W., 1926-   Holiday magic books.
GV1548.B3447 1990
793.8—dc20   89-8329
                                                                CIP
                                                                AC

Manufactured in the United States of America

1 2 3 4 5 6 7 8 9 10 98 97 96 95 94 93 92 91 90

CONTENTS

6

INTRODUCTION

Every March 17th, people of Irish ancestry all over the world celebrate St. Patrick's Day. They wear green, sing Irish songs, and dance Irish jigs. Some go to church while others go to parades. You can celebrate by getting your friends and family together for a St. Patrick's Day magic show!

There are many magical legends about St. Patrick. It is said that he chased the snakes out of Ireland and that he could make snow burn. They even say that the sun would not set for 12 days after Patrick died.

Does St. Patrick's Day magic really exist? It's up to you! Learn the tricks in this book and with the "luck o' the Irish" you can share the magical spirit of the day!

HOW THE SHAMROCK CAME TO AMERICA

HOW IT LOOKS

You show the audience two sheets of newspaper, roll each sheet into a cone, and place the two cones in two empty glasses. You show a paper shamrock and drop it into the cone in glass #1, which represents Ireland. Wave a magic shillelagh, or club, over the glass, remove the cone, and show both sides. The shamrock has vanished. Go to glass #2, which represents America. Remove the cone and show the audience that it contains the shamrock which vanished from the first cone. Tell the audience that this is how the shamrock came from Ireland to America—strictly by magic.

8

1. For this trick, you will need four sheets of newspaper, each cut into 12-inch (30-cm) squares.

2. Paste two of the sheets together, but leave an unpasted opening 4 inches (10 cm) wide across the top and 8 inches (20 cm) deep to form a secret pocket (**Figure 1**). Be sure to match the edges when you paste the newspapers together so that it looks like both sides of the same sheet.

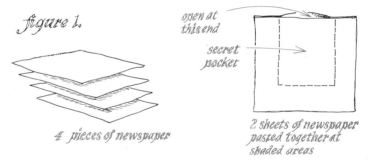

figure 1.

4 pieces of newspaper

open at this end

secret pocket

2 sheets of newspaper pasted together at shaded areas

3. Do the same with the other two sheets. You now have only two sheets of newspaper, each with a secret pocket.

4. From green construction paper, make two identical shamrocks, each about 2 inches (5 cm) wide (**Figure 2**). Put one into the sheet you will later insert in glass #2.

5. Make a magic shillelagh from brown construction paper (**Figure 3**).

6. Place two empty glasses, the two newspaper sheets (one secretly containing a shamrock), the other shamrock, and the shillelagh on a table.

HOW TO DO IT

1. Show the audience the two newspapers, roll the newspapers into cones, and place one cone in each glass. Make sure you put the cone with the shamrock into glass #2 — America.

figure 2.

shamrocks

2" wide

figure 3.

shillelagh

2. Show the paper shamrock to the audience and drop it into the cone in glass #1—Ireland. Actually you drop it into the secret pocket (**Figure 4**), but the audience doesn't know this.

3. Wave your magic shillelagh.

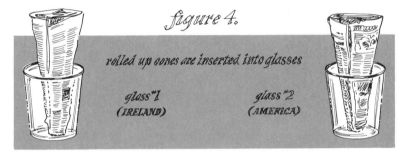

figure 4.

rolled up cones are inserted into glasses

glass #1
(IRELAND)

glass #2
(AMERICA)

4. Remove the newspaper cone from glass #1— Ireland—and show both sides. The shamrock has vanished.

5. Take the paper cone out of glass #2—America —and, without unrolling it, turn it over. The shamrock drops out. It has magically come over to America.

11

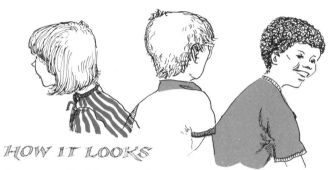

HOW IT LOOKS

As you divide a deck of cards in half and spread the two halves out, facedown, you talk about two Irish boys, Pat and Mike, who got lost. Have a volunteer from the audience take a card, "Pat," from one half of the deck, look at it, and place the card facedown in the other half of the deck. Have a second volunteer take a card, "Mike," from the other half of the deck, look at it, and place the card facedown in the first half of the deck.

12

You then square up the two halves of the deck, place one half on top of the other, and have the first volunteer cut the deck and complete the cut. Pat and Mike are now hopelessly lost. You tell the audience that since you are a magician you will find them. You look through the deck and drop two cards on the table. You have found Pat and Mike.

HOW TO MAKE IT

1. You will need a deck of playing cards, two slips of paper, and a pencil.
2. Ahead of time, put all the red cards—hearts and diamonds—together and all the black cards—spades and clubs—together (**Figure 1**).

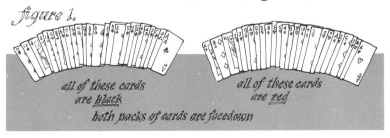

figure 1.

all of these cards are _black_

all of these cards are _red_

both packs of cards are facedown

1. Choose two volunteers from the audience and give each a slip of paper. Have the first volunteer write the name "Pat" on his slip, and the second volunteer write "Mike" on her slip.

2. Divide the deck of cards into two halves, looking at the faces of the cards without showing them to the audience. Put the red cards into one pile and the black cards into another pile. Spread the two piles out, facedown, on the table (**Figure 2**). As you do this, tell the audience about two Irish boys, Pat and Mike, who got lost.

you see the cards' color — the audience sees only the back of the cards

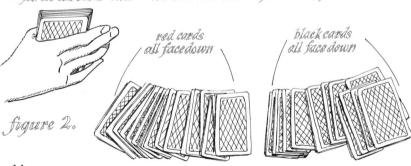

red cards all facedown

black cards all face down

figure 2.

3. Have the first volunteer take a card from one half of the deck and, without you seeing it, write the name of the card on the slip of paper marked "Pat."

4. Have the second volunteer take a card from the second half of the deck and, without you seeing it, write the name of the card on the slip of paper marked "Mike."

5. Have the first volunteer put his card, "Pat," facedown in the second half of the deck. Have the second volunteer put her card, "Mike," facedown in the first half of the deck.

6. You square up the two halves of the deck, place one half on top of the other, and have the first volunteer cut the deck and complete the cut. Pat and Mike are now hopelessly lost. Tell your audience that since you are a magician you will find the lost boys.

7. Look through the deck without letting the audience see the faces of the cards. You will easily be able to see which two cards were selected, that is, Pat and Mike. One will be a red card among the black cards, and one will be a black card among the red cards (**Figure 3**). Cutting the deck once should not disturb the order enough to lose the telltale positions.

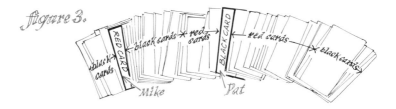

figure 3.

8. Pick out the two selected cards—Pat and Mike— and drop them faceup on the table. While the audience is looking at them, you casually pick up the deck and shuffle it a few times to mix the red and black cards. Explain to the audience that you found the lost boys by magic.

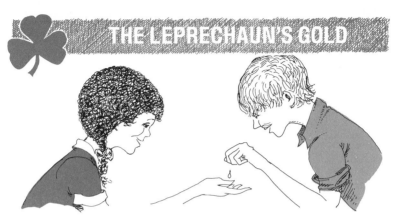

HOW IT LOOKS

You show a coin to your friend and say something like, "this coin is actually a gold piece that a thief stole from a leprechaun." Ask your friend if she knows what the leprechaun did when he discovered his gold piece had been stolen. When she says "no," ask her to hold out her hand, palm up. Hold the coin over her hand and squeeze it. Water drips down into her palm as you say, "The leprechaun cried and cried all day long."

17

HOW TO MAKE IT

1. For this trick, you will need a gold-colored coin. A foil-covered chocolate coin or a shiny penny will do, although a foreign coin would be better.
2. You will also need a small cotton ball. Dip the cotton ball in water and, without squeezing too much water out, conceal it behind your left ear.

HOW TO DO IT

1. You roll up your sleeves and show your friend that both your hands are empty, front and back.
2. Bend your left arm and place your left elbow on the table. This brings your left hand quite naturally to your left ear.
3. Pick up the coin with your right hand and begin to tell the story about the theft of the leprechaun's gold piece. Rub the coin on your left forearm (**Figure 1**) and ask your friend if she knows what the leprechaun did when he discovered his gold piece had been stolen.

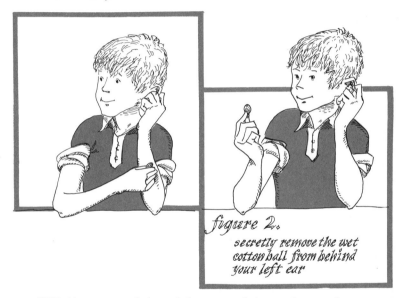

figure 1.

rub coin on
your left forearm

figure 2.
secretly remove the wet
cotton ball from behind
your left ear

4. While your friend is watching the coin, you
secretly remove the wet cotton ball from behind
your left ear with your left hand (**Figure 2**).

19

5. Transfer the coin from your right hand to your left hand. Keep the wet cotton ball hidden in your left hand as you cover it with the coin (**Figure 3**).

figure 3.

transfer the coin from your right hand to your left hand

cotton ball under coin

6. Ask your friend to hold out her hand. Hold the coin—and the wet cotton ball—over her hand and say, "The leprechaun cried and cried all day long."
7. Your friend will be startled and amazed when water—the tears of the leprechaun—drips into her hand.
8. You can then take the coin out of your left hand with your right hand and offer it for your friend to examine while your left hand with the cotton ball casually drops to your side.

HOW IT LOOKS

You show your friend a piece of paper with five squares on it. Place two paper shillelaghs on the two squares at the left end of the paper and two paper shamrocks on the two squares at the right end of the paper. Challenge your friend to make the shillelaghs and the shamrocks change places in exactly eight moves, no more and no less.

21

He is allowed two kinds of moves:

1. He can *slide* any of the four items into an empty space next to it.
2. He can *jump* any item over the item next to it, like a jump in checkers, provided he lands on an empty space.

While your friend probably won't be able to solve the mystery, you can do it in a few seconds because you know the secret.

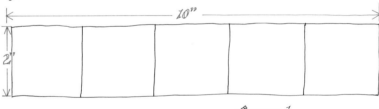

figure 1.

HOW TO MAKE IT

1. Cut out a piece of construction paper 2 inches wide by 10 inches long (5 x 25 cm). Draw lines on the paper, dividing it into five 2-inch (5-cm) squares (**Figure 1**).

figure 2.

1¾"

1½"

2. From cardboard, make two little shillelaghs and two little shamrocks. They should each be small enough to fit on a 2-inch (5-cm) square.

3. Place the shamrocks and the shillelaghs on the squares as shown (**Figure 2**).

figure 2.

place shamrocks and shillelaghs exactly as shown

Challenge your friend to make the shillelaghs and shamrocks change places in *exactly* eight moves. After he has given up, you solve the puzzle:

1. Slide the shillelagh into the empty space.

2. Jump the shillelagh with the shamrock.

3. Slide the other shamrock into the new empty space.

4. Jump that shamrock with the shillelagh.

5. Jump the other shamrock with the other shillelagh.

6. Slide the first shamrock.

7. Jump the shillelagh with the other shamrock.

8. Slide the shillelagh just jumped.

You have made the shillelaghs and shamrocks change places in exactly eight moves.

HOW IT LOOKS

Show a plastic glass half-full of green liquid, saying this is a glass of special St. Patrick's Day water. Shuffle a deck of cards and remove one card. Carefully place the glass of green water on the edge of the card and it balances there, even when you walk away from the table. You then remove the glass and show both sides of the card.

1. For this trick, you will need to fill a plastic glass half full of water and stir in a little green food coloring. This is your special St. Patrick's Day water.

2. You will also need a regular deck of playing cards.

3. Make up one special card which is in the regular deck. Paste half of a whole card onto the back of another card as shown (**Figure 1**). The loose flap of the rear card can be moved back by your thumb. This will hold the glass upright.

figure 1.

cards are pasted together at the shaded area

From the audience's view, it will appear that the glass of green liquid is balancing on a single card (**Figure 2**).

figure 2.

1. Show the plastic glass of green liquid to the audience and explain that it is special St. Patrick's Day water, which has some miraculous qualities.

2. Shuffle a deck of cards, keeping the special card with the fold-out flap on the bottom of the deck.

3. Remove the special card and, while trying to balance the glass on it, secretly fold out the flap with your thumb.

4. When you remove the glass from the card at the end of the trick, fold the flap back flat against the front card and show both sides of the card to the audience.

Note: You should practice this trick near a sink with plain (uncolored) water until you are sure you can do it without spilling.

MIKE, PAT, AND IRISH POTATOES

HOW IT LOOKS

Tell the audience a story about how two Irishmen, Mike and Pat, went into a store on St. Patrick's Day to buy some Irish potatoes. Even though it appears that each man is getting the same number of potatoes, Pat ends up with four potatoes and Mike has only one.

HOW TO MAKE IT

For this trick you will need seven pennies.

HOW TO DO IT

1. As you put one penny in your left hand, say that it will represent Mike.
2. As you put one penny in your right hand, say that it will represent Pat.
3. Tell the audience that the five pennies left on the table represent five Irish potatoes in the store.
4. Explain that Mike and Pat went into a store to buy Irish potatoes. They picked up potatoes one at a time. You pick up the five pennies, alternating between the right and left hand. *Be sure that you pick up the first penny in your right hand—Pat* (**Figure 1**).

5. You say the two men decided they didn't want potatoes after all so they put them back, one at a time. Put the five pennies back on the table, one at a time, *making sure that you put a penny from your left hand—Mike—down first*. You will now have two pennies in your right hand and none in your left hand (**Figure 2**).

figure 1.

pick up *first* penny with your right hand, then alternate between left and right hand

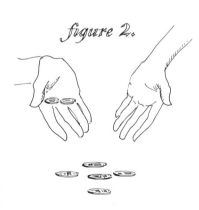

figure 2.

6. Now say the two men changed their minds again and decided they did want the potatoes. You pick up the pennies again, one at a time. Once again, *make sure the right hand (Pat) picks up the first penny.*

7. Now you open both hands and show two pennies in the left hand — Mike and one potato — and five pennies in the right hand — Pat and four potatoes.

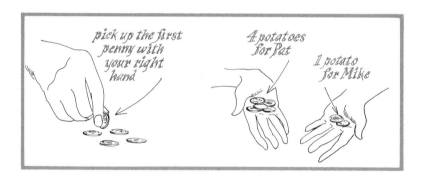

pick up the first penny with your right hand

4 potatoes for Pat

1 potato for Mike

8. Somehow, perhaps by magic, Pat got four potatoes and Mike got only one.

HOW IT LOOKS

You tell a story about how four Irish couples went to a St. Patrick's Day dance together, but soon got separated from each other. Along came an Irish leprechaun who waved his magic shamrock and magically put the four couples back together again.

1. For this trick, you will need eight index cards. Write one of the following names on each card and arrange the cards *exactly* as shown (**Figure 1**). From top to bottom, faceup, they should be: Mrs. Flannery, Mrs. O'Keefe, Mr. Flannery, Mr. O'Leary, Mrs. O'Brien, Mr. O'Keefe, Mr. O'Brien, and Mrs. O'Leary.

figure 1.

Mrs. Flannery — Mrs. O'Keefe — Mr. Flannery — Mr. O'Leary — Mrs. O'Brien — Mr. O'Keefe — Mr. O'Brien — Mrs. O'Leary

top ————→ *to bottom*

2. You will need to make a magic shamrock from a piece of green construction paper (**Figure 2**).

figure 2.

HOW TO DO IT

1. Tell your audience about the four couples going to the dance together and how they got hopelessly mixed up. Show the cards faceup.

2. Tell how the Irish leprechaun came along and waved his magic shamrock. Wave your magic shamrock over the cards.

top card to the
bottom –

next card faceup

top card to the
bottom –

next card faceup

3. Turn the eight cards over so the names are *face-down* and do the following:

    A. Put the top card on the bottom of the pack.

    B. Take the next card from the top of the pack and place it faceup on the table.

    C. Take the next card from the top and put in on the bottom of the pack.

    D. Take the next card from the top of the pack and place it faceup on the table, next to the first one placed there.

4. Continue this pattern—one top card goes under the pack, the next top card goes faceup on the table—until all eight cards are faceup in a line on the table.

5. The four Irish couples are magically back together to enjoy the dance.

HOW IT LOOKS

Tell your friend that the Irish believe in the power of the color green and that you will prove that there *is* power in green. Show your friend two glasses of water. One is clear and one is green. Drop a hardboiled egg into the first glass, the one with clear water. It sinks to the bottom of the glass and stays there. Lift it out with a spoon. Drop the same egg into the second glass, the one with green water. It sinks, but then rises to the top and floats, proving that the Irish are right. There is power in the color green.

37

HOW TO MAKE IT

1. For this trick, you will need a spoon, two glasses, some salt, green food coloring, and a hard-boiled egg.

2. Fill one glass three-quarters full with ordinary tap water.

3. Prepare a second glass as follows:

    A. Fill this glass three-quarters full with salt water, using one tablespoon of salt to each cup of water.

    B. Dissolve the salt by mixing thoroughly with a spoon.

    C. Add a few drops of green food coloring, just enough to turn the water green.

HOW TO DO IT

1. When you put the egg into the glass of clear water, it will sink to the bottom and stay there (**Figure 1**).
2. When you put the egg into the glass of green water, it will float (**Figure 2**). The salt in the water — unknown to the audience — makes the water heavier than the hard-boiled egg and so the egg floats. The green food coloring has nothing to do with the trick. It is just for misdirection.

figure 1.

glass filled with water
- egg sinks

figure 2.

glass filled with colored
salt water - egg floats

HOW IT LOOKS

While you turn your back on your friend, she holds a small picture of a shamrock in one of her hands and concentrates on it. You are able to tell her which hand the shamrock is in.

HOW TO MAKE IT

Draw a shamrock on a piece of cardboard about the size of a quarter.

1. Turn your back, then ask your friend to hold the shamrock in the closed fist of either her right or her left hand. Tell her to hold this fist by her forehead so she can concentrate on it.

2. Have her concentrate for about 30 seconds, then hold both closed fists out in front of her, side by side.

3. You turn around and look at her hands. You then tell her which hand the shamrock is in.

You will be able to see which of her hands is a little lighter than the other. The shamrock will be in the lighter one. This is because the blood in the hand holding the shamrock will have drained down from the hand while she was holding it up by her forehead.

41

COUNTIES OF IRELAND

You show the audience seven index cards, each with the name of an Irish county written on it. Ask them to remember as many of the counties as they can. Lay the cards facedown on the table and ask people in the audience to call out the names of some of the counties written on the cards. Write the counties called out on separate pieces of paper, fold the slips, and drop them into a paper bag. When finished, take the index cards into the audience, hold them facedown, and allow someone to select any card. Put the rest of the cards back on the table. After mixing the slips in the paper bag, have someone reach in and pick any slip. When the slip is unfolded, the place on the slip matches the place on the index card.

1. Ahead of time you must make up two sets of index cards. On one set, type or print the names of the following places—Dublin, Galway, Kildare, Limerick, Kerry, Tipperary, and Waterford—all counties in Ireland (**Figure 1**).

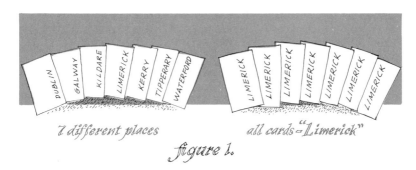

7 different places   *all cards="Limerick"*

figure 1.

2. On the other set of seven cards, type or print "Limerick" on each card. Be sure that all the "Limericks" look exactly alike, the seven on the second set of cards and the one on the first set of cards.

43

3. Before your performance, hide the second set of seven cards — all with "Limerick" on them — behind some prop on your table.

4. You will also need a paper bag, seven slips of paper, and a pen or pencil.

HOW TO DO IT

1. Show the seven cards with different place names on them slowly, one at a time, and ask your audience to try to remember them.

2. Walk back to your table and casually lay the seven cards down on the table behind a prop.

3. Ask the audience to call out the place names they remember seeing on the cards so you can write them down.

4. As the place names are called out, you write each one on a separate piece of paper, fold it, and drop it into the paper bag. (Actually, you just *pretend* to write down the different names called out. You *really* write "Limerick" on every slip.)

5. When all the place names have been called, set the paper bag aside and pick up the seven index cards. You *really* pick up the second set of cards, all with "Limerick" typed or printed on them, although the audience thinks you have seven cards all with different places on them.

6. Offer the cards facedown and have one selected. (It will be a "Limerick" card.) Put the remaining six cards back on your table.

7. Shake up the paper bag and have one of the folded slips taken out of the bag by a member of the audience.

8. Have the person unfold the slip and call out the name of the place. It will be "Limerick," the very same name as on the card selected.

9. Tell the audience they have just witnessed an Irish miracle.

TRICKS FOR BETTER MAGIC

Here are some simple rules you should keep in mind while learning to perform the tricks in this book.

1. Read the entire trick several times until you thoroughly understand it.
2. Practice the trick alone or in front of a mirror until you feel comfortable doing the trick, then present it to an audience.
3. Learn to perform one trick perfectly before moving on to another trick. It is better to perform one trick well than a half dozen poorly.
4. Work on your "presentation." Make up special "patter" (what you say while doing a trick) that is funny and entertaining. Even the simplest trick becomes magical when it is properly presented.
5. Choose tricks that suit you and your personality. Some tricks will work better for you than others.

Stick with these. *Every* trick is not meant to be performed by *every* magician.

6. Feel free to experiment and change a trick to suit you and your unique personality so that you are more comfortable presenting it.

7. Never reveal the secret of the trick. Your audience will respect you much more if you do not explain the trick. When asked how you did a trick, simply say "by magic."

8. Never repeat a trick for the same audience. If you do, you will have lost the element of surprise and your audience will probably figure out how you did it the second time around.

9. Take your magic seriously, but not yourself. Have fun with magic and your audience will have fun along with you.

ABOUT THE AUTHOR

James W. Baker, a magician for over 30 years, has performed as "Mister Mystic" in hospitals, orphanages, and schools around the world. He is a member of the International Brotherhood of Magicians and the Society of American Magicians, and is author of *Illusions Illustrated*, a magic book for young performers.

From 1951 to 1963, Baker was a reporter for *The Richmond (VA) News Leader*. From 1963 to 1983, he was an editor with the U.S. Information Agency, living in Washington, D.C., India, Turkey, Pakistan, the Philippines, and Tunisia, and traveling in 50 other countries. Today Baker and his wife, Elaine, live in Williamsburg, Virginia, where he performs magic and writes for the local newspaper, *The Virginia Gazette*.

ABOUT THE ARTIST

George Overlie is a talented artist who has illustrated numerous books. Born in the small town of Rose Creek, Minnesota, Overlie graduated from the New York Phoenix School of Design and began his career as a layout artist. He soon turned to book illustration and proved his skill and versatility in this demanding field. For Overlie, fantasy, illusion, and magic are all facets of illustration and have made doing the Holiday Magic books a real delight.